Hour of the Poet

Goldfish Press

Seattle

Hour of the Poet

(Thoughts upon the Lake of Time)

Poetry by

Lewton Thomas Jones

Copyright © 2015 by Lewton Jones
All Rights Reserved

Published by
Goldfish Press, Seattle
2012 18th Avenue South
Seattle, WA 98144

Manufactured in the United States of America

ISBN 978-0971160163
Library of Congress Catalog Card Number 2015936874

--- Dedicated to my Father ---

Contents:

Two Black Cats and a World in Chaos   p.8

Helena   p.10

Ashland   p.11

The World Outside   p.12

Last Time at the Rover   p.13

House in the Rain   p.15

Conversation with a Neighbor   p.17

River House on the Pacific   p.19

Jane's Place   p.20

My Father's Warehouse   p.22

The Brutes that Destroyed Beauty   p.23

Colorado Memory   p.24

Divorced   p.25

Price to Pay   p.26

Astoria #2   p.27

Jet to Cabo   p.28

Bells of Saint Marks   p.29

Mother   p.30

Cabo San Lucas   p.31

Night of Providence   p.32

When My Eyes No Longer See   p.34

I Learn from the Sea   p.36

The Buildings Watch   p.37

Loneliness   p.39

5000 Dollar Summer   p.40

Herman Lake Arapho Colorado   42

Alaska Moment   p.44

My Granddaughter Almost Seen   p.45

Trees Remember   p.46

Astoria   p.47

February Blue   p.49

Two Black Cats and a World in Chaos

Two black cats and a world in chaos

One Called Finnegan and the other Blackie La Chat

They saunter and swagger through my ranch style house

Feasting on fish, chicken livers and cheap half and half

Around the corner is a boarded up drug house

Up the street lawns get better - a cult ti sac cadenza

Catnip is like heroin to felines; they flip and flop in lost abandon

I surf the channels and see a head amputation on the news

Proof that no one is safe even the NRA

Tails of lions tales of distal culture mayhem

Our drones will get them back or a good fracking

I log on to Facebook, Outlook, Twitter Look, Linked in, You Tube and Netflix

Slamming the mouse down as I go, as Nintendo minions create new passwords,

New jargon, and impossible passwords for baby boomers to snag

My cat steps on the keyboard just as I spot a quick craigslist job

I need nine more lives to pay back my student loans!

I need more Twinkies and Plaid Pantries to get the money for rent

I drift out on the couch in the TV radiation light curled like a cat

Sleeping on top of my pipe dreams lofty shelf

Like a leopard up a tree

Helena

My prairie falcon would wait on high above me

In a yearling's ecstasy we chased the fleeing prey

We hunted together in the honeyed fields of lore

My first falcon, the King's Bird

A downy princess from the cliffs of John Day

She dropped like her parents 200 mph

A majestic site harmonizing the Icarus zenith

We traversed as two, the golden shawl of nature

Feathered thyme lit earthly raptured hills

A bright spot in time comforting my sad young soul

Her godly flights of impossible ending

Silver bells ringing mirth to Merlin

A castle song in a world of shadows

My overseer to the broke earth below

My first and only symphony

Ashland

My hope in the park is an acorn

A nugget of Summer's pride

We sit under soft lilting greenery

Basking in prophetic quietude

I sleep-watch one leaf float away

Summer is exiting again

Our blind dissonance and unrequited love

Chill the warm day

We struggle for hope and compensation

Soon we two will fade like Shakespeare

Othello winds and winter tales

No matter what we do or say

There will be other days

And seasons of decay.

The World Outside

Cold and homeless USA

The poor litter our nation today

Hope is a tool in the hands of monsters

An epidemic of greed and narcissism

Our love our lives are hopeful endeavors

Lined up like elephant skins

I think the brontosaurus should speak up

The thunder lizards have had their way far

Too long

Last Time at the Rover

A Free Freckled infant sees me

We watch his little stick walk

Supine strangers on the river beach way

It's the end of Summer September 22nd 1996

Summer is my best friend

The sun glows into a parallax view of scarlet light

A coda supreme

A windy sigh fills the trees by the hushed river

The tender blue sky yields to fall

I am 45 years too young to say goodbye to joy

Rooster Rock is the place to go for daydreaming

We watch the moving boats, jets, gulls and crows

A soft celebration of nothingness

I am here merely counting time in the sand Time's

quick candle wavers from the breath of life

Once warm now a windy chill

Out on the river's table

Reluctantly adhering

To Autumn

House in the Rain

I have a house that sits out in the rain

A rainbow sits upon my weather vane

The street outside my door

Has no name

And all the people passing by

They look the same

Back in my memory a younger man I see

With lovely ladies

A Chinese watercolor is my sky

With cherry water and the light in someone's eye

The roses bloom rich red and sweet green fills the air

Like a ship inside a bottle it's always been there

I go outside sometimes to places far and near

And when the clouds pass by

The water forms a mirror

I have a house that sits out in the rain

The past is filled with joy and also pain

A rainbow sits upon my weather vane

Conversation with a Neighbor

    My father she said

    Was a piano player

    A scientist

    From New York

    He moved to the Catskills

    Right after he bombed Nagasaki

    I Brave Thomas

I brave Thomas made my mark

As time raced Secretariat

Children grew to men families moved

Many of my friends changed

With their hearts on loan and jobs denied

A generation of love like no other kind

Some were pure to the end

Some thought love was money

Flipping without shame

Some just wanted a piece of me

To own everything thing they could see

We all carried sins to last a lifetime

A Greek Tragedy never waking

I only had to play my part

River House on the Pacific

Sunset steals our days away

Darkness settles on the town.

Spreading its black cape behind the stars,

Flickering and quivering brightly,

The moon glows silver princess sweet.

Thor's pale fire dome no longer pulsates

Souls wander ghost- like in abbeys, lost

Shadow cast into deception's nocturne void,

A milky white saucer, floating in time and space, gyros

Spinning vanity's plate into a lonely recall,

Deep blue water rings echo estuarine promise

To an undertow of creatures lost,

A window from the café glows in the clinks and rattles

As Loch Ness shadows appear in hidden perfection outside,

Our window of uncertainty.

Jane's Place

Love once upon a time

Or so it goes

They tell me anxiety

Hampers your ability to remember things

Yet I remember you

And love

The rent was 75 dollars

A buckled house on Southeast Main

A place for our coyote dogs

Zelda and Kievik

You gave the place to me

Went back to San Francisco

Babe came over to stay

You and your chestnut brown swirled hair

Lean legged blue jeans and hippie work shirt

Hipper and funnier than anyone

We drank and sang as Laurie played piano

Two beautiful kids staying out of trouble

A thousand umbrellas could not stop the rain

My Father's Warehouse

My father's warehouse is filled with rough tools

Scattered dusty artifacts worn smooth from hard work

Arid honest sunlight streams golden ropes of hope

Through the old gray windows where cobwebs glow

Forklifts and pickups stand ready in their faded painted nodes

A concrete floor spreads out to begin labor and steady income

Steel scaffolds are stacked up leaning onto receding walls

Old twisted grainy wood steps rise to second and third floors

My father's warehouse unlike my rock n roll poverty is real

It is not self-serving it is much tougher,

It sacrifices time

To help the rest

No matter the climate or the assignment.

The Brutes That Destroyed Beauty

The brutes that destroyed beauty

Would claim our history unabashed

With ghost songs in the fractal sky

The lost gravitational idioms

Crawl by like polluted streams

Still waiting

War-speak slurs us with genocide and murder

Destinies to interrupt scourged and cut

The swords of putrid nations

Loki tyrants continue to wreck us

Erroneous scripts of false consciousness

Now become their lost satanic fields of justice

Clawing and breaking us with cruel tools

The cult of fame with headlines for bloodlines

GENETIC STRIDING MONSTERS ABOUND

Colorado Memory

Screaming teacher vacuum cleaner

Meat loaf for dinner

Unable to draw stars on the American flag

My unfair punishment

Do it over and over and over again

I ran home past musty dusty cattails

A milkweed trail past plum trees and corn fields

My only friends

No solace

Returning to our haunted driveway

Where

The stream ran free across the road

I lit the field on fire not much later

Streams and keep out lakes

Sliced through my armor

Whipped by my father's belt

Divorced

I am here again

Older

I stand to say goodbye to

My once held wife and princely son

In this state

Where I once gathered obsidian with Mexican friends

Ancient earth knows I was intelligent

Price to Pay

My poetic hereditary dialect is poesy, intuition and mystic tribulation

There is a price to pay being this way, leaving the pack behind

To a road leading me to nowhere you think is important

My love lost is stacked away in guarded memory

May the sun blast the influenza valley

Speed away baby I am lost and eager to love another day

There is a real price to pay for walking out from all this

Faces frocked with gout and TB consumption

Push to shove scream to glove

You stand out in grand abandon

We are free original-sinless

A younger innocence

A glow

Above

The rest.

Astoria #2

She danced logic on the rain pane flotilla

Sun fell on arrival in low tide Astoria

The radio played jazz lines

Behind café glass and wallpaper halls

W/Hermes sealed inside Slothville's hip lil alleyways

Night came on more than coldly in Empty Town Endura

Bye bye love,

Telephone deliver me

Answer me true

She loves only

You.

Jet to Cabo

The sun chimes weightless

Above my January room

Steady as Tierra Del Fuego

I'm thirsty for laurels

Hungry for prove all

Amid slick deception

Walking river city w/ winos and pale tattoos

I lay quick-lilted

Marooned in orbit

Sacked by the cool day shuffle

Marking sharp circles round Blue Death

Her shiny emporium is silver thawed

By heaven's hot optic star.

Bells of Saint Marks

The endless song of rain

Pats the glass roof lightly

The church I was wed pulsates holiness

Gregorian drives the mass in a world that never ends

Bells ring on time across the day

We begin to begin again and live for forgiveness

While some drink wine for honesty

Some drink for regret

Some for the divinity

Some to destroy everyone they have met.

Mother

I remember my mother burning tumble weeds

In yard piles with wicker basket pride

Flower /bent she fought our poverty

Raking and clawing the burnt cutgrass,

weed malaise where we all played

An ozone smell always came before the exploding rain

It fell like syrup from the black Colorado sky

In our desolation far from the TV eye

She wielded hope

Like Joan of Arc

Cabo San Lucas

Subtle serpent suns itself lulling souls into a peaceful appetite We are intoxicated by warm gardens as Mexican angels guard The unanswered paradise an airline route away

A wandering child fresh from the ocean wakes me
He asks- are you in this dream too?
It is Equator hot where wealth morphs the rancid barrios Marina fiesta, bonita siesta, broken piñatas, destiny's sha grin Thousands of cactus crowns bloom in emerald aloe groves Everyone stops as they hear gun shots down the road

A scarlet blood dance ensues without warning
No past, no present, no future awaiting

Nights of Providence

Lime green winter lies frozen cracked

In the nazi night glass

Her blue breath fogs the pop sickle ceiling

She says call me Aurora Borealis

I step out from view inisolationabandondment

Lonely inandout

Weholdtobeone

Smooth bodies

Temporal bliss

Last night's wind blew sad

I walked Crab Road in soft Christmas light

Rain fell into the sea mist sleep

Dark fire storms

Uneasy ghosts

A nervous sky

These are the nights of providence

Of promises lost

Purpose at any cost

Catch the moment-see me

For the future will lose me

Why is love a bedfellow to misery?

A homely mistaken importance

The end of you and me

When my eyes No Longer See

The world holds true

A child is nurtured

My unique pathos is angst alive

In this atomic painting

Life and death keep moving

With or without me

Always and forever to be joined

To earth and sea

Soon to be a body pale

Sunlight glimmers as ghost-angels pass

Gliding fast to light the mother lode-faire

When my eyes no longer see I won't hear

Dull whisperings from passing cars

Only music from children playing

Green growing grass above this box

Bursting daffodils anew

Here now every new day

Known before it is through

Eternity to see

Breathed in breathed out-existence

The eye is a peak-hole to

The whole of darkness

Lost light knows the void

I Learn From the Sea

I learn from the young

I learn from the sea

I built my net worth from a design

Of vernacular tea

It was a blueprint of desire

A template writ in time

The disease is not in me imperialistically

It's in the twelve steps half wept apologies

The seeds of society

I walk alone and break free

With anyone who gets free

Even scotch and whiskey must someday

Join the sea

The Buildings Watch

This town is a down, down, down town

It feels like the buildings have watched me

As I lurked the streets of my youth

From heartache to heart breaking jive

Dour feelings conquered me

This town leaves no traces or faces to

Its whereabouts and care-abouts

Only clear empty dreams and rain parades

The repetition of sour seasons unbreakable

Sarcasm and corn pone conformity

In time I became just another anomaly

Winners smiling seratipiciously

Waving to anybody up a tree

All the while the highway called to me

Racking my brain

For one small victory

I unfortunately

Have never been Free.

Loneliness

I awoke from a caffeine-amphetamine explosion

Overdosed at 2 with my brother Danny

We survived

The breath of life came back into cool days waiting

Sackedslaphappyhyperactivity

Our new false optimism

A slip noose waving

When I feel this lonely - kick the chair

Vacant inside for years

Holding on to family, friends, time, earth

And consequence

5000 Dollar Summer

I charge the running streets of recoil and containment

All green lights it seems, 20+ lime lights flashing new heralds

My thirst for connection

Thoughts lost in merry metaphor

Sleeping on my laurels realizing everything has gone

Then sudden inspiration******

Sitting at the seashore remembering my lines

The lost imploding waves

Vacuum space

Rolling presence

I Am Water Too

I hear the call like tempered clouds do

Its China blue September

Light halos gold patterns

Indescribable hush

A panther silence

God blows smoke rings around this open fishbowl

Is Merlin here too?

Does Neptune know we are watching?

Herman Lake Arapho Colorado

As children we wore blue cutoffs-shirtless

It was Denver 1958, the green Summer of our Packard

We drove to Lake Herman to swim and play

I remember running after we parked down to the lake

My mother forged through the dirty water beside me

Suddenly she recoiled and cried out in pain

She had stepped on a broken bottle in the murky silt

Her artery was severed- clearly by the amount of blood

Coloring the water like a red dye

She screamed in pain her anguish stopped everything

My glee was silenced the trip turned to tragedy

Much like when my brother Danny chopped his finger deep

With a butcher knife while carving on wood

Koda Crome tragedies all from unknown circumstance

Sitting in wet cutoffs we drove to the hospital

Another time another zone not televised

The Korean War had just ended.

Alaska Moment

Earth/hearted wolf is tireless

Beaten but unbowed

True to moon and timeless air

Calling out a blue hue howl into our primal eternity

If trapped he will eat his foot off

For his liberty in the tundra

His pack is spotted as guns fire their thin line humanity

With pride and elation the chase is on

All run towards the cover of trees

One wolf stops glares up at the copter above

To confront, to protect the pack, a snow Spartan's last stand

Then an act of instant cruelty, he is struck down

In safety, the swirling pilot masters fly way

HE WAS BRAVER

My Granddaughter Almost Seen

My Granddaughter almost seen,

Still not born before any memory or thought

She was to be tall and free

I saw her in my dream,

My son's bright lithe sprite

Her head was crowned in gold

Like my daughter in law's sweet soft heart

My Granddaughter almost seen is above this valley

Passing in loveliness and laughter

Her silver light spirit passed like a song

In the sullen night,

A whisper of her own design

Each year to grow taller to frolic in the sand

A gilded lily on memory's flowered road

Stepping lightly to heaven

Trees Remember

Trees remember years of spun slumber

Chlorophyll blood drives a swaying leaf's entropy

Trees recall years of raging cold and solar caress

Nerves in reverie hatch snakes sky bound

Sending wood through earth, rock and clay Trees never forget the time or day

Always steel tender they remember the gentle way Every year mark rings of arbor genesis

Forests of tall children standing free on earth

Ageless entwined bound together forever Like giants thoughts.

Astoria

Green table linen

Cadmium note book

Pink French sea

Fade too grey

Day dream ends as we parted

Sorry is love beneath water

The Mainland of Hope

The Mainland of Hope

Glistens

Its rocky shore beckons lost souls

Gulls fly over albatross wed

Upon green tides spraying the blue knolls

The cliff towers float like phantoms

In the pallid fog

Charcoal clouds swirl in the moon's cauldron

The Mainland of Hope is lost space in waiting

We sail to her shores weary

As harbor blue canaries greet us

We arrive love's marina and take aim

The heat of the day and the breath of the sun are her targets

February Blue

Inside each and every flower colors begin

Inside every color oceans might end

I became a better man when I forgave my father

Still the living press on in this February blue

Moss and mildew permeate the basement air

There are blossoms on my apricot tree-too early

A murder of crows charge the winterized sky

Gentrified weather on a green globe warming

A refrigerator floor drips out of control

The Dow Jones is peaking again

But consumer confidence is wanton

As hundreds of thousands lose their jobs

The dreams of the few are the nightmares of the many

A money pot fattens as the lottery bong chaaaa-chinnngs

Hollywood posers lie in the sun imitating imperfect lives

In hopes of winning an Oscar with their car crash facelifts

Hair Piece ads and gaudy jewelry motivators sell cable

Babbling non sequiturs on voyeur reality show fables

Infantile segues from people you really don't want to know

A Star Search parade of emotionally monistic hits

A Who Knows Who and What the Hell is there to do Charade

Shadows down the street huffing paint thinner and airplane glue

Crack the high ball merriment without a clue

After All, All that is, Is February Blue

Lewton Thomas Jones is a musician and teacher. He has done graduate work in English and this is his second book.

www.ingramcontent.com/pod-product-compliance
Lightning Source LLC
Chambersburg PA
CBHW031504040426
42444CB00007B/1208